THRU
the WALL

RODGER EPLEY

Outskirts Press, Inc.
Denver, Colorado

A gift for

From

Table of Contents

Dedicated

TO GOD, TO JESUS CHRIST,
AND TO MY SPIRITUAL GUIDES WHO
PROVIDED ME WITH ETERNAL LOVE AND
GUIDANCE THOUGHOUT MY JOURNEY OF DISCOVERY

Acknowledgement

A special thanks to Frances Cooper for her selfless act of kindness to be of help and encouragement in writing this book. I couldn't have done it without her.

Illustrations by the author, Rodger Epley

Prelude

"OH MY GOD, WHATEVER IT IS, IT'S COMING THRU THE WALL," and the room was illuminated with a radiant gold and white blinding light. "What in the world is this?" "Is this a dream?" Her goddess-like appearance and mystical air of brilliance were being revealed from the other dimension, and she was breathtakingly beautiful in her DIVINE way. There was absolutely no fear in me, and her response was in PURE LOVE! She was proudly showing all of her incredible grandeur and heavenly splendor along with the story she brought from the other side.

This is my story. What I just told you is true. An event that was unexplainable and unlike anything I have ever experienced before. For those of you who have never met me, I am an honest and sincere person from the old school, where your "word is as good as gold and your handshake is trust." This remarkable story will electrify you to feel the LOVE that was brought from the Spirit World.

"IN ORDER TO WRITE ABOUT LIFE, YOU FIRST MUST LIVE IT."
—Ernest Hemingway

 A few stories have been written for you to see my life as it progressed along the winding road from a boy through middle age to the prime of life. As we venture through this "DIVINE PHENOMENON," you will feel the LOVE that is unlike the physical LOVE that we know.

"TRY NOT TO BE A PERSON OF SUCCESS, BUT RATHER A PERSON OF VIRTUE."
—Albert Einstein

WHERE THE BUFFALO ROAM: The time was winter in a small rural town in Kansas. The Spirit World had decided that this location was an excellent place for me to spend some time in learning of the development called LIFE. Blistering hot in the summertime and bitter cold in the winter, with the blizzards blowing across the prairies like you have never seen before. Tumbleweeds would roll across the roads and cling to the barbed wire fences giving you the feeling of an old Western movie. Then when the wind changed they would roll in the other direction.

One would have to drive through Kansas when driving from the state of Missouri, the "show me state," to the "colorful state of Colorado." Both of these states are beautiful vacation states, and the impression that Kansas may leave with a traveler is, "Will I get to see an Indian?" or "Is this where the buffalo roam?" But this is the home of Dorothy and Toto, together with the Wizard of Oz, who lives at the end of the yellow brick road. This is my home, and this is the land where I grew to be the person I am today.

"FAITH SEES THE INVISIBLE, FEELS THE INTANGIBLE, AND ACHIEVES THE IMPOSSIBLE."
—Anonymous

COUNTRY DOCTOR: On a cold blustery day in December, I was in the operating room in this small-town Kansas hospital. This was one of the first memories of my life, and I can remember the only two employees in the operating room. The nurse was wearing one of those high-front nurse's hats that were worn before the war, and the old country doctor had on the long white doctor's coat that hung almost to the floor. The country doctor wasn't gentle, was unsympathetic, had no patience, and it was apparent that he didn't want to be there. Mother kept saying, "Take a deep breath and you will be OK!" The doctor was annoyed with kids, and he didn't have the time to explain what was happening as he went through the tonsil removal procedure. A "no patience" doctor – that's for sure! – and I can remember the ether mask being placed over my face, and the smell of ether with the drip drip drip of the drops until my mother's face began to fade away. The reality of life and my spiritual adventure were just beginning in this small-town hospital! The reward of ice cream seemed to smooth the moment.

"MAN'S REAL LIFE IS HAPPY, CHIEFLY BECAUSE HE IS EVER EXPECTING THAT IT SOON WILL BE SO."
—Edgar Allan Poe

RUSTY NAIL: How lucky it is to be born in a privileged generation, to experience similar events from our parents' lives that reflect on our current lives. My parents were not fortunate enough to enjoy the modern medicine and procedures in their days that we had. "See this hand?" my father said as he held up his hand. His finger had grown closed and his hand was crippled. "This happened when I was a boy when I fell down the stairs and caught it on a rusty nail," he said. "The pain was unbearable and to see a doctor was out of the question, so I just learned to live with it," he said. That was prairie life in those days, and "LIVING" was rough and raw and "courage" was out there for everyone to experience. "It is courage, courage, courage, that raises the blood of life to crimson splendor. Live bravely and present a brave front to adversity." – Horace.

"THE FIRST AND FINAL THING YOU HAVE TO DO IN THIS WORLD IS TO LAST IN IT, AND NOT BE SMASHED BY IT."
—Ernest Hemingway

THE MIRACLE CREAM: The magical formula was Mentholatum Ointment that Dad and Mom used on everything that moved or didn't move. It made no difference if the injury was serious or not, Mentholatum was going to be used one way or another. My life was saved by this miracle medicine until I learned that it was only a slight local anesthetic. The main ingredient was camphor, a soothing ointment, and Mother had me covered with it from head to toe for bites, scratches, cuts, bruises, and even athlete's foot. She would say, "Up the nose for colds" and "Rub your chest down" at bedtime. And believe it or not, Mentholatum was discovered and manufactured in Wichita, so there was always plenty to go around.

"IT IS A COMMON EXPERIENCE THAT A PROBLEM DIFFICULT AT NIGHT IS RESOLVED IN THE MORNING AFTER THE COMMITTEE OF SLEEP HAS WORKED ON IT."
—John Steinbeck

MY TOWN, USA: No longer were there rumors of war. It was wartime, and "anxiety was in the air." The actual time had arrived and we were kept informed by the radio between anxieties. Some were listening to the Great Gildersleeve to relieve tensions. Other stations were tuned to Amos 'n Andy and Fibber McGee & Molly. Lives were turned upside down because women had to go to work doing men's jobs. Never in this age have we seen such change. Limited gasoline and sugar were available. This was not an enjoyable period of time. Many of the town folks were driving to Wichita for employment in the aviation field to support the war. The streets were active with the rumble-seat cars driving the old red brick streets. I could feel the sadness with the local folks along with the soldier men and women preparing for overseas duty. "Wars may be fought with weapons, but they are won by men. It is the spirit of men who follow and of the man who leads that gains the victory." – General George S. Patton

"FROM HIS CRADLE TO THE GRAVE, A MAN NEVER DOES A SINGLE THING WHICH HAS ANY FIRST AND FOREMOST OBJECT SAVE ONE – TO SECURE PEACE OF MIND, SPIRITUAL COMFORT, FOR HIMSELF."
—Mark Twain

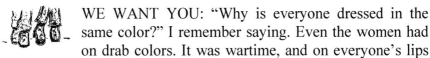 WE WANT YOU: "Why is everyone dressed in the same color?" I remember saying. Even the women had on drab colors. It was wartime, and on everyone's lips was talk about the fighting. Men were seen standing in lines at the recruiting office to sign up for the service. Dad was in the National Guard at the time, and I can remember the uniform he put on and how fearless he looked. Mother took us down to see Dad giving cadence to the soldiers, and I watched them march in step to this loud commanding officer who was shouting instructions. The noise the marching boots made on the wooden floors was loud and powerful. In a few days, the unit shipped out to Europe and all was quiet again except for the radio that carried the news of the war.

"ONCE YOU SAY YOU'RE GOING TO SETTLE FOR SECOND,
THAT'S WHAT HAPPENS TO YOU."
—John F. Kennedy

THE LONG BROWN ENVELOPE: Father was a tall proud giant of a man and life was not always easy. The fact that he walked 13 miles a day carrying mail wasn't nearly as difficult as delivering the long brown envelope, the "missing in action" letter. Many times he would say that this was the hardest part of his job.

"FAR AWAY IN THE SUNSHINE ARE MY HIGHEST ASPIRATIONS. I MAY NOT REACH THEM, BUT I CAN LOOK UP AND SEE THE BEAUTY, BELIEVE IN THEM AND TRY TO FOLLOW WHERE THEY LEAD."
—Louisa May Alcott

 I LOVE YOU, MOTHER: "I love you, Mother!" This is the second time that I told my mother "I love you" because those were unspoken words in our family. Deeds were more important than words. The words that were never spoken came so easily now that my mother was ill. Why do we wait so long to use the beautiful words "I love you." Her eyes sparkled as though she knew I had always felt the love between mother and son. I don't know why it is so hard to say those "three little words" that really come out very easily once you get used to saying them. Mother, I want you to hear me say to you, and for you to always know that "I LOVE YOU, MOTHER!"

"ONE OUGHT NEVER TO TURN ONE'S BACK ON A THREATENED DANGER AND TRY TO RUN AWAY FROM IT. IF YOU DO THAT, YOU WILL DOUBLE THE DANGER. BUT IF YOU MEET IT PROMPTLY AND WITHOUT FLINCHING, YOU WILL REDUCE THE DANGER BY HALF. NEVER RUN AWAY FROM ANYTHING. NEVER!"
—Sir Winston Churchill

THE CAVE: Returning for a visit to my hometown, I find myself standing in front of the old homestead, reminiscing of days gone by. Flashbacks of friends and relatives come and go and forever become history. This was where the neighborhood cave was created and has long since been filled in. The cave was dug in the backyard and was deep and dark with tunnels in all directions. My brother, along with the neighborhood boys, placed straw on the floor and lined burning candles along the sides of the cave. Cardboard was placed across the top of the cave and then covered with a light layer of dirt to make it look natural. Everyone was crawling on their hands and knees to see and feel how dark and cool it was, and you could see how proud the boys were over their creation. They were charging five cents for the neighborhood kids to crawl through it, and they were served lemonade at the end. The lemonade I remember not only had a satisfying sweetness but was touched with a tint of pink. Childhood was carefree with no fear. Over the cave now sits a beautiful home that was built without knowledge of "the cave," and the young boys who built the cave may have gone on to become the Frank Lloyd Wrights of the future.

"THE FRAGRANCE OF THE VIOLET SHEDS ON THE HEEL THAT HAS CRUSHED IT."
—Mark Twain

FIRST MEMORIES: Now is the time for my memories to be put on paper, and writing the recollections of my past is a delightful experience. My memories during the first steps of growing up and developing to where I am today are significant to me. Recalling the details makes it easier to write about them, and as time passes, how delightful it is to remember the little stories. Only I know of these treasured memories in the way they happened to make them so valuable. This is the moment before they vanish forever.

"CHARACTER CANNOT BE DEVELOPED IN EASE AND QUIET. ONLY THROUGH EXPERIENCE OF TRIAL AND SUFFERING CAN THE SOUL BE STRENGHENED, VISION CLEARED, AMBITION INSPIRED, AND SUCCESS ACHIEVED.
—Helen Keller

 BUBBLEGUM BOY: The price was one cent and the name was "bubblegum," and it was introduced around school with everyone trying to see how big of a bubble they could blow. The girls were waiting for me to show them how it was done, but I had never tasted bubblegum before and it tasted sugary and luscious. And I knew I was going to be embarrassed with all of the girls watching me, and I was, but it was exciting to finally blow a bubble after a day of practice. The excitement of bubblegum came and went, and now came the toothpick dipped in cinnamon oil. "Boy did that burn the lips." But it was cool-looking to have one dangling from your lips, and to have the little bottle in your jeans to be able to offer one to everybody. The cinnamon sticks were almost as good as the Sin Sin Licorice.

"I LOVE THE MAN THAT CAN SMILE IN TROUBLE, THAT CAN GATHER STRENGTH FROM DISTRESS, AND GROW BRAVE BY REFLECTION."
—Thomas Paine

 CRANK IT UP: We were all shocked to see Dad sitting in front of the house with a large grin on his face, honking the horn. It was a Model T Ford and Mother said, "Com' on, gang, it's Dad's new toy." The wheels had wooden spokes and it had to be hand-cranked to start it. I can remember Dad saying, "Careful, you can break your thumb." "Cup the crank handle in your palm rather than placing your thumb over the top of the handle." I can remember how thrilled we all were to have something that moved so we wouldn't have to walk. It was exciting to ride in the backseat and have everyone see me when we drove down the street. There was no air conditioner or heater in the car, but we never noticed it. Mother was always complaining about the price of gasoline at 19 cents per gallon. Bread was 8 cents a loaf at the time and milk was 34 cents a gallon. "Boy, were those the good old days!" "To get the full value of a joy you must have somebody to divide it with." – Mark Twain

"THE MAN WHO HAS DONE HIS LEVEL BEST, AND WHO IS CONSCIOUS THAT HE HAS DONE HIS BEST, IS A SUCCESS, EVEN THOUGH THE WORLD MAY WRITE HIM DOWN A FAILURE."
—B. C. Forbes

 LITTLE RED WAGON: Mother was pulling and I was pushing the little red wagon down the street to our new home. The wagon was full of books and we had six blocks of dirt roads to go, and Mother was wearing her sun bonnet and I was barefoot with ragged jeans and a hand-me-down shirt. There appeared to be thousands of sandburs in front of us that I kept stepping on. Like a minefield that I'd see in war movies. No, these were not sandburs, they were goat heads, I learned, with the two or three sharp-pointed stickers. Oh, they hurt as a boy, and Mother kept pulling them out and I would wipe the drop of blood away and then take a few more steps before pulling another one out. The sand was deep and hot and I had the joy of new sights and smells along the way. As we crossed the bridge, I can still smell the black tar and the cut alfalfa. How exciting to meet our new neighbors and their pretty little daughter that was my age. She was sure cute, but my little red wagon was prettier.

"I AM SEEKING, I AM STRIVING, I AM IN IT WITH ALL MY HEART."
—Vincent Van Gogh

RIDING THE RANGE WITH HOPALONG: One of the very first things that we did upon arriving at our new home was to tie an old tire on a rope and hang it from the cottonwood tree for a swing. We named this rubber horse "Hopalong," and it swung during the bitter winds of winter and through the scorching heat of summer. For hours and hours, this was the excitement that the neighborhood kids and I had. Hopalong and I rode the range and fought many battles with Indians and mosquito bites. He was privileged to be ridden by many greats like Gene Autry, Roy Rogers, The Lone Ranger, and Tom Mix. It was figured we had to ride 350 swings to make the 5,380 feet in a mile ~ we rode many a mile!

"GIVE WHAT YOU HAVE. TO SOMEONE ELSE IT MAY BE BETTER THAN YOU DARE TO THINK."
—Henry Wadsworth Longfellow

NATURE BOY: "Nature Boy" was one of my nicknames in school. It had to be because "I loved animals and birds" and was always seen reading books on nature and wildlife. The bird songs were the most intriguing, and I was constantly whistling and imitating their calls. When asked to do a birdcall like the "mockingbird" or "cardinal" call, I would immediately start into the whistling presentation. The love of nature has followed me through life, where I am still drawn towards the love of nature's little friends. If asked now what one adventure I would like to have before my life is completed, my answer would still be the same as it was when I was a boy: "to soar like an eagle."

"WHEN YOU HAVE DECIDED WHAT YOU BELIEVE, WHAT YOU FEEL MUST BE DONE, HAVE THE COURAGE TO STAND ALONE AND BE COUNTED."
—Eleanor Roosevelt

 FIRST YEAR OF SCHOOL: The old wooden floors creaked and moaned when the teacher strolled by my desk in school. Each step she took would be frightful, and the ruler she carried in her paw was to slap our hands if we were not good. "How would you like to have this thing for your mother?" I said to my friend. And then there was recess, where we would lie down on our little blankets to relax. "Relax with this thing roaming around the room – no way." Never will I forget the girl who had the desk next to me and how pretty her legs looked when she was standing with her back to me. I can't believe I was noticing this at my age. These legs looked better than my little red wagon. I would just stare at them, and I couldn't wait to get to class every morning just to see them. Must be a man thing, I guess. Oh, how I wanted to just touch them. So I figured if I could just drop something on the floor, then I would be closer to them when I picked it up. I was determined to go through with this, and my heart was beating so fast I couldn't breathe. Off the top of the desk went the piece of paper, and it floated back and forth down to the floor and landed just back of her legs, and "Now is the time, go for it," I thought. When I bent over to pick the paper up, I touched the back of her leg with my arm. "I did it! WOW, I did it!" She turned and looked at me, and I nonchalantly looked away. "An adventure well accomplished," I thought.

"EXAMPLE IS NOT THE MAIN THING IN INFLUENCING OTHERS. IT IS THE ONLY THING."
—Albert Schweizer

THE MISSING CHOCOLATE BAR: INTEGRITY and HONESTY were two important words that I learned at an early age. It was without thinking that I picked a chocolate bar up in a store and silently slid it into my pocket without paying. When Dad found out that I'd stolen the candy bar, he didn't have a smile on his face and the tone of his voice changed. "Go back and tell the owner what you did and pay him five cents," he said. The owner was more embarrassed than I was, and my eyes were on the floor when I told him. The owner gave me the candy bar and I learned well the words "INTEGRITY" and "HONESTY."

"THE MORE I GIVE MYSELF PERMISSION TO LIVE IN THE MOMENT AND ENJOY IT WITHOUT FEELING GUILTY OR JUDGMENTAL ABOUT ANY OTHER TIME, THE BETTER I FEEL ABOUT THE QUALITY OF MY WORK."
—Wayne Dyer

SPARE THE ROD: Our family was built on "respect," and our parents disciplined us by the "spare the rod" verse that didn't "spoil the child." When my father spoke, we listened, because it was "respect" speaking. The truth was always told to my father because I loved him and respected him. There was only one incident that I can remember receiving punishment from him for that I deserved, and that was when I kicked my younger brother below the belt. He firmly said, "Come over here. Now turn around," and wow, do I remember how hard he hit me on the seat. "Example is not the main thing in influencing others. It is the only thing." – Albert Schweitzer

"A WOUNDED DEER LEAPS THE HIGHEST."
—Emily Dickinson

 HOT MILK, COLD HANDS: Milking the cow was my job before and after school so we could sell the milk to the neighbor for ten cents a quart. In the summertime, the cow's tail was always hitting me in the face because of the flies, so I had to spray before milking. It was really a bad day when the cow stuck her foot in the bucket, but Mother understood. When I got older I would hold the bucket between my legs when milking, but at this age it had to rest on the ground because of my size. An interesting item that I learned about milking is that a cow has five tits but only the front four give milk, and that is where the old saying "worthless as the fifth teat" comes from.

"MY MOTHER SAID TO ME, 'IF YOU BECOME A SOLDIER, YOU'LL BE A GENERAL, IF YOU BECOME A MONK YOU'LL END UP AS THE POPE.' INSTEAD, I BECAME A PAINTER AND WOUND UP AS PICASSO."
—Pablo Picasso

CONTENTED FELINES: When milking, what an enjoyable event it was to see the five cats we had patiently waiting in line for a free hot meal straight from the cow. They would come a running for a position when I started milking and would line up for the hot milk that I would squirt at them. It was quite comical to see five cats all in a row licking milk off of each other and being happy with a free meal. Interesting as it may seem, the mouse population always stayed high with the cats so well fed.

"THE BEST REMEDY FOR THOSE WHO ARE AFRAID, LONELY OR UNHAPPY IS TO GO OUTSIDE, SOMEWHERE WHERE THEY CAN BE QUIET, ALONE WITH THE HEAVENS, NATURE AND GOD. BECAUSE ONLY THEN DOES ONE FEEL THAT ALL IS AS IT SHOULD BE AND THAT GOD WISHES TO SEE PEOPLE HAPPY, AMIDST THE SIMPLE BEAUTY OF NATURE."
—Anne Frank

FOUR-LEAF CLOVER: Are there real four-leaf clovers? Yes, and they have their own individual aroma, so that once you smell them you won't forget it. The normal clover has three leaves, and after picking hundreds and maybe thousands, you may just find one with four leaves. To lie down in a clover patch and look for one is so exciting, and you may just get lucky and find one. The four-leaf clover is the sign of good luck. What do the leaves symbolize? One leaf is for FAITH... The second for HOPE... The third for LOVE... And the fourth for LUCK. In Irish tradition, the three-leaf clover represents the HOLY TRINITY: one leaf for the FATHER, one for the SON, and one for the HOLY SPIRIT. The fourth leaf represents GOD'S GRACE. The mystique of the four-leaf clover continues today and is a rare occurrence of GOOD LUCK.

"GOD SELLS US ALL THINGS AT THE PRICE OF LABOR."
—Leonardo da Vinci

THE COLOR YELLOW: The SUNFLOWER grows wild in Kansas, and you can see a sea of yellow for as far as the eyes will take you. The sunflower can be found growing along roads, in gardens, and in parks, and it is also harvested for "sunflower seeds." It is the state flower and is the flower that is used romantically to pull the petals off individually and repeat, "She loves me, she loves me not." The last petal pulled off would cause either the happy or the unhappy face. Counting the petals first in secret and knowing what the outcome would be was my cup of tea!

"I THINK AND THINK FOR MONTHS, FOR YEARS. NINETY-NINE TIMES THE CONCLUSION IS FALSE. THE HUNDREDTH TIME I AM RIGHT."
—Albert Einstein

PRAIRIE FRAGRANCE: Early in life I was aware that prairie flowers, fruits, and vegetables had their own unique fragrance. The dusty smell of wheat being harvested was very distinctive, along with the soy beans and the freshly cut corn. Most of the vegetables from the garden, like the cantaloupes and cucumbers, had their own stimulating aromas and could be identified if you were blindfolded. Peaches made me think of this special girl at school. Pears from Grandmother's pear pie. The purple stain from the mulberries and the gooseberries made me shiver. The noise the watermelon made when they would split it open after cutting, and mashed potatoes fresh from the garden after digging them. To quote a saying from Mohandas Gandhi, "To forget how to tend the soil is to forget ourselves."

"MAN HAS BEEN ENDOWED WITH REASON, WITH THE POWER TO CREATE, SO THAT HE CAN ADD TO WHAT HE'S BEEN GIVEN. BUT UP TO NOW HE HASN'T BEEN A CREATOR, ONLY A DESTROYER. FORESTS KEEP DISAPPEARING, RIVERS DRY UP, WILD LIFE BECOME EXTINCT, THE CLIMATE'S RUINED AND THE LAND GROWS POORER AND UGLIER EVERY DAY."
—Anton Chekhov

TROUBLED: It takes no effort to kill, and it was an immeasurable mistake when I was a boy. Killing is so simple and easy that you don't think about it at the time. My parents bought me a rifle for my fourteenth birthday and I killed a rabbit, and you wouldn't know the emotion I felt! My creator and I have been in correspondence together in asking for forgiveness for taking away part of nature. Who am I to take an animal or bird's life? Anyone can pull a trigger. I cannot tell you how ashamed I felt! My father gave a speech where he said, "I am disturbed with killing, it bothers me." My older brother, giving the eulogy at Dad's funeral, said, "Dad told me that he didn't like to stop a heart no matter what its size." My father's footsteps cannot be duplicated, but they can be admired.

"THIS IS COURAGE IN A MAN: TO BEAR UNFLINCHINGLY WHAT HEAVEN SENDS."
—Euripides

LIP FISHING: One of my joys in life as a boy was fishing in the creek on the farm. My hands were so cold one time that I didn't want to reach in my pocket to get my pocketknife, so my teeth were used to bite the fishhook line to change hooks. This is normal for a fisherman to do instead of finding his knife. At this time I was standing on a fallen tree when I slipped and fell and ran the fishhook through my lip. "Can you believe this, a fishhook caught in my lip?" How embarrassing it was to walk into the doctor's office with a fishhook stuck in my lip and sit in the hospital lobby with everyone watching me. The doctor ran the hook completely through my lip and cut the end off. This story couldn't wait to be told and spread through school as the cartoon of the year.

"TO WISH TO ACT LIKE ANGELS WHILE WE ARE STILL IN THIS WORLD IS NOTHING BUT FOLLY."
—Saint Teresa of Avila

UP IN SMOKE: "FIRE, FIRE, the garage is on fire!" Mother was trying to put the fire out in the middle of night with the garden hose, and it looked like she didn't have a chance from the beginning – and she didn't! Fire engines and sirens were everywhere along with the townspeople, and it was an exciting and scary event. Puff ~ my little red wagon is gone and it went up in smoke with all of the memories we had together. A bright new shiny bicycle replaced the little red wagon, and we immediately started new journeys with new memories.

"IF WE ARE FACING IN THE RIGHT DIRECTION, ALL WE HAVE TO DO IS KEEP ON WALKING."
—Ancient Buddhist proverb

WALKING THE DIRT ROADS: Miles and miles of dirt roads led in all directions from our farmhouse. Kicking and throwing rocks and just enjoying walking the dirt roads with my friends were some of the best times of my life. It was a feeling of freedom and a good time for quiet thinking and problem-solving, watching and listening to the birds, animals, and insects while breathing the dust from the dirt roads when a car passed. We chased grasshoppers that were plentiful, and there were thousands of wildflowers to be picked for their beauty and aroma. Our shoes were always dirty, but our minds were always carefree and happy.

"GREAT THINGS ARE NOT DONE BY IMPULSE, BUT BY A
SERIES OF SMALL THINGS BROUGHT TOGETHER."
—Vincent Van Gogh

 CHASING FIREFLIES: Only on the farm would I see
unusual incidents that normally wouldn't happen in the
city. The absence of city lights made it easy to see the light
of the firefly or glowworm. Catching them was a favorite pastime.
As I held them in my palm, they showed me their luminescent glow
on and off. I always thought they would bite you or burn your hand,
but they are safe and a fun memory. Once they are caught and placed
in a bottle, you have a ready-made night lantern. After they showed
their lighting display, the jar would be opened and away they would
fly to demonstrate once again their lightning exhibit in the dark of
the night.

"I COME TO THE OFFICE EACH MORNING AND STAY FOR LONG HOURS DOING WHAT HAS TO BE DONE TO THE BEST OF MY ABILITY. AND WHEN YOU'VE DONE THE BEST YOU CAN, YOU CAN'T DO ANY BETTER. SO WHEN I GO TO SLEEP I TURN EVERYTHING OVER TO THE LORD AND FORGET IT."
—Harry S. Truman

GRANDDAD: Granddad was quite a guy and would always make us willow whistles from a backyard willow tree. When we were being ornery, he would cut a willow switch and carry it down his pants, showing some of it just to frighten us, but I can't remember him ever using it. He helped me fly a kite one time and the kite went almost out of sight. It went so high that people drove by to see who was flying it and where it originated from. The kite was made in the shape of a star and was painted red, white, and blue and flew majestically when the wind lifted it to the clouds. We would write notes on pieces of paper and attach them to the string and send them up to the kite. Yes, my girlfriend's name went up the line more than once with a secret message, only to break loose with the secret message lost in the clouds forever.

"THE PRIMARY CAUSE OF UNHAPPINESS IN THE WORLD TODAY IS . . . LACK OF FAITH."
—Carl Jung

 HERE COME THE CHICKENS: "Here they are," I would yell excitingly. Boxes and boxes of baby chickens had just arrived from their long trip. The chicks were peeking through the round holes in the box awaiting their new home, so off we went to watch them scatter in all directions searching for food and water. They looked to be the size of a fifty-cent piece, and I would lie down on the straw under the light to watch and feel the little chicks running up and down my arms and legs, a memory never forgotten. My new title that was given to me was very important: "manager" of feeding, watering, and watching for "the fox of the barnyard."

"EDUCATION IS HANGING AROUND UNTIL YOU'VE CAUGHT ON."
—Robert Frost

THE OLD COTTONWOOD TREES: We could depend on our magical cottonwood trees, which told us that a storm was approaching with the song it would sing with the wind blowing through the leaves. The cottonwood tree is the state tree of Kansas and a native tree for many prairie birds and squirrels. Many times on a stormy night, the breaking of the limbs on the rooftop would awaken us. The trees told us that the storm was upon us, and we all headed for the basement. Mother was afraid of the spiders and mice in the old basement, but down we went to huddle with the "jars" of Mother's beans and tomatoes. She showed more fear of the mice and spiders than the storm.

"I AM LIKE A LITTLE PENCIL IN GOD'S HAND. HE DOES THE WRITING. THE PENCIL HAS NOTHING TO DO WITH IT."
—Mother Teresa

SWIMMING IN THE CREEK: My parents thought at the time that it was OK to swim in the creek, so I considered myself a lucky person to have such a cool water hole to chill down in. The dirty water with the crawling things and the cuts and scrapes, scuffs and bangs, bumps and smacks, bashes and sunburns were memorable. The water felt so good, and we would dam up the creek to make the water higher, and then we would relax and "take a dip" with the frogs. It was fun to swim under a frog and grab its legs and pull it underwater, and I would always let it go. The cows liked to stand in it, and every animal came to the creek for a drink and to cool off in the summer heat. Now if I were asked to return to the creek for a dip, I would likely say, "PERHAPS."

"WE SHALL LIVE TO FIGHT AGAIN, AND TO STRIKE ANOTHER BLOW."
—Alfred Lord Tennyson

RAILROAD TRACKS TO WHERE? The train track curved next to our farm, and standing close to the tracks thrilled us. The old black steam engine would barely be moving with the black smoke filling the air, and the noise of the working engine was deafening. We would lay a penny on the track and after the train passed, run up to the track to find the smashed penny that was still hot. "What a thrill!" The smashed penny would be carried in my pocket, and I would keep taking it out to relive the time and place. "Oh how I would like to play Huckleberry Finn and see where the train goes." But we knew that when the little red caboose went out of sight the feeling was gone for the day, only to return at another time.

"FIRST THERE ARE THOSE WHO ARE WINNERS, AND KNOW THEY ARE WINNERS. THEN THERE ARE THE LOSERS WHO KNOW THEY ARE LOSERS. THEN THERE ARE THOSE WHO ARE NOT WINNERS, BUT DON'T KNOW IT. THEY'RE THE ONES FOR ME. THEY NEVER QUIT TRYING. THEY'RE THE SOUL OF OUR GAME."
—Bear Bryant

THE MARBLE KING: The big game that the boys constantly played on the school ground was the game of marbles. It was a big thing in school at this time, and this may be because there was so much dirt to play in and everything wasn't paved with concrete. I always had my bag of marbles and was ready to play any time I would be challenged. I practiced and practiced every day in my spare time to aim and shoot that marble as hard and accurate as I possibly could at those beautiful shining marbles inside the circle, just waiting to be won by me. The large slick colorful shooter was my king marble, which I used to try to knock the other kids' marbles out of the ring that we drew in the dirt. I always seemed to have fewer and fewer marbles in my bag at the end of the day because I must have had a hole in the bag.

"HE TURNS NOT BACK WHO IS BOUND TO A STAR."
—Leonardo da Vinci

I MUST GO DOWN TO THE CITY DUMP, TO THE WONDERFUL DUMP IN THE SKY. AND ALL I ASK IS A GARBAGE TRUCK AND A STAR TO STEER HER BY: On a lazy afternoon, one of my favorite pastimes was to go to the city dump. Mother would say, "He brings back more than he takes out." There were so many interesting things that could be found by just digging through the mountainous pile of orange peels far away from the city's life. Many of the little "treasures" that I would find and drag home would be antiques now. Broken toys from earlier years were brought back to life and reborn again. When I took home jewelry one time, Mother became enthused real fast, and the time I took home an old gun excited Dad.

"THE MIDDLE OF THE ROAD IS WHERE THE WHITE LINE IS, AND THAT'S THE WORST PLACE TO DRIVE."
—Robert Frost

MIDNIGHT TRAIN TO FLORIDA: At the early age of twelve, my folks sent me to Florida to live with my grandparents for the summer. The time was the early 1950s, and apparently my parents felt a twelve-year-old could make the trip by himself. "WOW, was this a long trip to travel all this distance," I thought. The train left from Wichita, Kansas, with a five-hour layover in St. Louis, Missouri, and then down to Jacksonville, Florida. It was a scary moment for me at the St. Louis terminal with this long layover, and the terminal looked liked pictures I had seen of Grand Central Station. I sat on the wooden benches for five hours and met many interesting people who were surprised that a twelve-year-old boy was making such a trip. It was an exciting journey sitting in the dome car on top of the train and sleeping on the train with all of the stops it made along the way. It was scary at the time, but a quality memory now.

"THE DIFFERENCE BETWEEN GETTING SOMEWHERE AND NOWHERE IS THE COURAGE TO MAKE AN EARLY START."
—Charles M. Schwab

SATURDAY NIGHT TREAT: Dad would start up the old 1936 Chevrolet to head to the ice-cream store for the Saturday night treat. He was working the floor gears and gunning the engine with excitement. Eating out was unheard of when I was a boy because we didn't have the money for such luxuries, so we all looked forward for the family to go together. Ice-cream bars were five cents each, and I always got one with nuts on it. The others were always quarrelling over the colored popsicles. What a treat this was, and maybe, just maybe, an order of french fries to go with it. The windows were rolled down and the summer breeze was hot and dry, and the cold taste of the ice cream was delicious but never enough.

"LIFE SPENT MAKING MISTAKES IS NOT ONLY MORE HONORABLE BUT MORE USEFUL THAN A LIFE SPENT DOING NOTHING."
—George Bernard Shaw

BUCKING BALES: "Bucking bales," or pulling square bales of alfalfa up onto a flatbed and then unloading them in a barn, was the work that built the body. An iron hook was used to hook the bale so you could handle the bale, and at the end of a day your body felt like mush, but you got up the next morning and continued on into the day until the body got into condition. Tractors didn't have enclosed cabins at this time, and the driver would have to suffer the weather and worry about going to sleep and falling off the tractor.

"WE SHALL GO ON TO THE END. WE SHALL FIGHT IN FRANCE, WE SHALL FIGHT WITH GROWING CONFIDENCE AND GROWING STRENGTH IN THE AIR, WE SHALL DEFEND OUR ISLAND, WHATEVER THE COST MAY BE. WE SHALL FIGHT ON THE BEACHES, WE SHALL FIGHT ON THE LANDING GROUNDS, WE SHALL FIGHT IN THE FIELDS, AND IN THE STREETS, WE SHALL FIGHT IN THE HALLS. WE SHALL NEVER SURRENDER."
—Sir Winston Churchill

UNUSUAL FOR SURE: "Unusual to say the least" was summer employment at the small-town cemetery in my hometown. This piece of real estate had to belong to the hundreds of striped ground squirrels that occupied and owned the rights to live and play on the grounds. The work gave me an opportunity to look for "sayings and quotations" for a research paper I was working on in school. The number one saying was "GROW OLD ALONG WITH ME THE BEST IS YET TO BE." The oldest dates were in the 1700s and barely readable, and some had wooden sticks that were used as markers. One man was buried with the only love in his life, his 1930s car. Not my favorite place to spend an afternoon of leisure, but an interesting remembrance.

"THE GREAT THING IN THIS WORLD IS NOT SO MUCH WHERE WE ARE, BUT IN WHAT DIRECTION WE ARE MOVING."
—Oliver Wendell Homes

LOVE OF THE OUTDOORS: It was the summer of '57, and being employed by the State Quail Farm was a totally new experience for me. Thousands of baby quail and pheasants were hatched in incubators and then raised to maturity before being released in the wild. This was a state program to increase the population of the quail, a small game bird plentiful in the Midwest. One incident I always remember from this place was an employee slipping on one of his knee-high rubber boots and saying, "I feel like I may have something moving under my sock." So he pulled off the boot and out ran a mouse. This was a short funny incident that always stayed with me.

"ONE LEARNS BY DOING THE THING; FOR THOUGH YOU THINK YOU KNOW IT, YOU HAVE NO CERTAINTY UNTIL YOU TRY."
—Sophocles

MUST I? My music world was disastrous! It was terrible, and I drove everyone insane with this instrument I was playing called the "violin." Every mouse in the neighborhood was at attendance with the noise I was making, and I pictured them all on their haunches sitting around in a circle. This started at a very young age when I was constantly asked, "Why the violin?" Because it was the only musical instrument left in the house that no one wanted to play. The other two instruments went to the brothers that snatched them up and left only the violin. So off to music lessons I would go twice a week to play in orchestra, and the only boy playing the violin. It was miserable and continued for five years. The violin was broken in numerous places and had to be glued back together, but I kept playing it. On the way to practice one day and being as discouraged as I was, I threw the violin under a bridge. I was sure lucky that it was still there when I returned.

"OPTIMISM AND HUMOR ARE THE GREASE AND GLUE OF LIFE. WITHOUT BOTH OF THEM WE WOULD NEVER HAVE SURVIVED OUR CAPTIVITY."
—Philip Butler
Vietnam POW

 WHAT IS A SNIPE? "Come go snipe-hunting with us," my so-called friends said one night. So out to the country I went to go snipe-hunting, to hold a bag with another sucker in the corner of a field to catch a bird called a snipe. There is a bird called a snipe, but they are hunted like any other game birds, and they are not going to run into a bag at night. It takes two dimwits to hold the bag open in the dark while the other people go to the other side of the field and line up and start towards the bag, allegedly to drive the snipes into the bag. So here comes the gang making all kinds of noises, and you think that they are scaring the birds in your direction and that shortly the bag will be full? "What a joke." So I held this bag for what seemed to be hours until I heard the group coming across the field making all sorts of noises. I just knew the bag was going to be full soon, and we were told each snipe was worth twenty-five dollars. "Keep checking," I would say to my other buddy, who was constantly feeling the bag. "We're going to be rich," he said. Well, I never caught a snipe that night and I never got rich, but I have this everlasting memory of holding this sack in the corner of a wheat field late one night.

"MANY OF LIFE'S FAILURES ARE MEN WHO DID NOT REALIZE HOW CLOSE THEY WERE TO SUCCESS WHEN THEY GAVE UP."
—Thomas A. Edison

BE PREPARED: What an exciting time it was for me growing up and being a member of the Boy Scouts, and how motivating it was to be an instructor. I taught classes in cooking, proper dressing, etiquette, and survival in preparing them for later life. Their motto was important because it covered many subjects we would need for better living throughout life. You can see how significant each word is from their motto: "Trustworthy, loyal, helpful, friendly, courteous, kind, obedient, cheerful, thrifty, brave, clean, and reverent." These are encouraging words for a boy to learn the meanings of and to grow old with throughout his life.

"TRY NOT TO BECOME A MAN OF SUCCESS, BUT RATHER A MAN OF VALUE."
—Albert Einstein

DOING A GOOD DEED: My folks always wanted me to accomplish one good deed a day in helping others. And I found it easy! That is the name of the game here on earth, and trust me, you will experience a warm sensation with a high feeling of accomplishment. They say the SOUL is located behind the heart area, and everything we do while here on earth is recorded and will be replayed. As a boy I tried to be good to others, but I didn't try hard enough. Oh how I wish now that I had packed that recorder full of good deeds so that they might be played and listened to at a later date. It's never too late to receive that "GOLD STAR FOR THAT GOOD DEED."

"YOU PRAY IN YOUR DISTRESS AND IN YOUR NEED;
WOULD THAT YOU MIGHT ALSO PRAY IN THE FULLNESS
OF YOUR JOY AND IN YOUR DAYS OF ABUNDANCE."
—Kahlil Gibran

FIELDS OF GOLD: What a thrill! My first combine ride, and excitement is in the air. This was my first trip to Western Kansas during the summer with the windows down and the hot air blowing through my hair. As we stepped out of the car, the combine was making its way towards us. "Run along the side and jump on," someone yelled to me. The combine wouldn't stop, but would slow down just long enough to hop on. There was a sense of "hurry up" in the fields to "keep on cutting" before the rains. The clouds were a shade of green that indicated rain, and damaging hail was approaching. Everywhere you looked, the wheat was being cut with as many as six combines in a row, cutting swaths through the yellow gold. All of the farmers had serious looks on their faces, and they were all working overtime threshing wheat and filling elevators. There was so much wheat this year that the elevators were filled to capacity, and it was being unloaded on the ground like towering pyramids. Cutting would continue until the sun went down and long afterwards into the night. The tired, dusty-faced men had reached their goal before the storm. WOW, what an adventure this day had been, and I had been a small part of it!

"I'M A SLOW WALKER, BUT I NEVER WALK BACK."
—Abraham Lincoln

TO FLY AGAIN: It was a Kansas blizzard, and I was tagging along on a hunting trip with my brother and friend.

We sighted this goose in the middle of a pond, and to get close enough for a shot, we would need to crawl along a tumbleweed fence. There would be one shot with the rifle, and one shot only, since the goose would be gone after the noise. We started crawling on our hands and knees through ice and snow. My hands felt like they were frozen but I kept going, and after we had crawled as far as we could, my brother and friend each wanted to take the shot. "I want to take the shot," my brother kept saying. After arguing they ended up flipping a coin, all of this in a blinding snowstorm, and my brother won the flip and took the shot and shot slightly over the goose's head. The goose lifted off the water and was gone in seconds, and I was happy to see it fly into the blizzard and disappear in the distance.

"WE HAVE GRASPED THE MYSTERY OF THE ATOM AND REJECTED THE SERMON ON THE MOUNT."
—General Omar N. Bradley

THE GREEN LIGHT: The time was early evening and I was in this western Kansas town spending the summer with my grandparents. This place is "GOD's country," and many evenings after the cow was milked, we would walk down to the railroad station to see the train come roaring through town. WOW, did it come through!!! The depot was a small building along the tracks with two rows of wooden benches and a small window to buy a ticket. This was a picture right out of the Old West. We would stand on the track until the light turned green and listen for the noise and rumble of the distant train to appear. "Put your ear on the track and you can hear it coming," someone said. "The light is green, here it comes," we would yell. And when it came through town it was deafening, and the depot shook like an earthquake. A mail bag would be thrown off and the train wouldn't stop unless there was a passenger to board. What a thrill to see the conductor waving his night light and the approaching train. Then, all was quiet again except for the usual night sounds of the prairie.

"LIFE IS NOT COMPLEX. WE ARE COMPLEX. LIFE IS SIMPLE, AND THE SIMPLE THING IS THE RIGHT THING."
—Oscar Wilde

GRANDFATHER: Grandfather was from the "Old Quaker" line, and he came out west from Pennsylvania. "Nothing but heat and wheat" and "No matter what you do, always tell the truth," he always said. He looked old and wrinkled with his snow-white hair and soft-spoken voice. He would have fit in perfectly with a scene from Christmas since he had the twinkle in his eye and was giving of himself. I remember that special time sitting on the porch swing when he handed me a catalog and said, "Pick what you want, boy." So I chose a tiny photo viewer, and I walked to the post office and mailed the order. The post office was a couple blocks down the dirt road, and each day I was allowed to go by myself to check the box and see if my little package was there. I was disappointed that there was nothing in the box the next day, so every day I made the walk and finally, there it was in the box, the little plastic toy. I was so thrilled and excited. What a happy time of my life, and what a difference a twenty-five cent gift made in those days.

"BELIEVE, WHEN YOU ARE MOST UNHAPPY, THAT THERE IS SOMETHING FOR YOU TO DO IN THE WORLD. SO LONG AS YOU CAN SWEETEN ANOTHER'S PAIN, LIFE IS NOT IN VAIN."
—Helen Keller

NEW MARSHAL IN TOWN: Patrolling the garden was my job and I saw to it that all animals were put on notice that the barefoot boy with the weather-beaten shoes and worn-out jeans was the "new marshal" in town. Band-Aids covered my body like Indian war paint. It was my time to learn how to plant a garden and how to cut a potato with an eye on each piece. Mother also had me "snapping beans" for canning, a very simple procedure where the bean is broken in two or three places. Long green cucumber vines were interwoven along the ground. "Don't plant cucumbers and cantaloupe together," my father said, "because the bees would cross-pollen and the cantaloupe would taste like skunk scent." This is a true statement. Every year I would have my own watermelon patch to see if I could win the "King of the Garden" award. "Buy the largest Black Diamond seeds you can find," I was told. "And have them ready to plant come spring." These "black beauties" were being watched not only by me, but along with many animals like the raccoon. They knew how to get to the lush red flesh by carving a hole through the rind and then reaching in with their little hands for a feast. Several times I have gone to the patch and found every melon destroyed by this masked desperado. Then it was "wait until the smaller melons matured so we could compete again for the King of the Patch." Ahh . . . life in the garden as a law man!

"MY CROWN IS CALLED CONTENT; A CROWN IT IS THAT SELDOM KINGS ENJOY."
—William Shakespeare

PRAIRIE PETS: My first wild animal pet that I had, other than the dog or cat or barnyard animal, was the ever inquisitive raccoon. He was an orphan, and I found him looking for food down in the pasture. He sure liked the sand plums I gave him and followed me home for more! I had to make a tradeoff with Mother for keeping him for running the sweeper. He was constantly going through my pockets, looking for food and washing it before eating it. They are very clean and inquisitive, and their eyes are constantly moving with their black masks around their eyes like the mask of Zorro. My next pet was a cute little black-and-white pet skunk that was also an orphan. Because of the ever-so-popular skunk's fragrance, I was sent home three times from school. Mother would have to bury my clothing to erase the odor, and I spent quality time in the bathtub.

"TO KEEP A LAMP BURNING WE HAVE TO KEEP PUTTING OIL IN IT."
—Mother Teresa

"OUCH!" The woodpecker hole in the cottonwood tree was very active with the comings and goings of the red-headed woodpeckers. Something was going on there and I was going to find out. For a week I had been watching this activity, so I got the ladder and reached in the hole and found three baby woodpeckers. I was excited about raising one for a pet, so after watching them grow day by day, I finally reached in the hole and "ouch," something bit my finger and drew blood. So I got a ladder, and lo and behold, there was a baby opossum looking at me with his two big eyes. What a surprise! So now I had a baby opossum for a pet and Mother said "NO." Being bitten should have sent me for a shot, but in those days we just moved on with our daily activities.

"THE GREATER THE OBSTACLE, THE MORE GLORY IN OVERCOMING IT."
—Moliere

BARBED WIRE FENCE: Every direction you looked you saw barbed wire fence. It was said that the barbed wire fence helped to win the West, and we all got injured at one time or another trying to crawl through it. The wire would rip your shirt or pants and then draw blood if you weren't careful with it, and it was a miracle that I never got a serious injury from the rusty sharp barbs. The electric fence came along after the barbed wire fence and would give a jolt of electricity if you were bold enough to touch it. And by touching the person you were with, you would pass the "shock" to them. A cow would know the fence was there after past encounters and would test it once with its tongue and then "up goes its tail."

"MAKE US HAPPY AND YOU MAKE US GOOD."
—Robert Browning

 FAITHFULL DOGS: "GO" was the word they both knew. Both were rat terriers that would follow me everywhere I would go step for step. These were my two best pals that were always tagging along behind me. Off to the pasture they would race when hearing that word "GO." They would run out a ways and then turn around and sit with their tongues hanging out. Take another step towards them and they would start off again. The farm had a weed patch called the "Jungle" that was full of eight-foot-tall weeds, and this was where I had my own little hide-a-way to escape also. The dogs knew where to find me and would come charging through the weeds barking all the way. I have thought many times how nice it would be to have another "jungle" to return to.

"REFLECT UPON YOUR PRESENT BLESSINGS, OF WHICH EVERY MAN HAS MANY; NOT ON YOUR PAST MISFORTUNES, OF WHICH ALL MEN HAVE SOME."
—Charles Dickens

 THE BROKEN WING SHOW: We have a neat little bird living on the prairie called the killdeer. Although the killdeer are technically in the family of shorebirds, they may be found a distance from water. They love to nest in gravel, and the nests are hard to find unless you search for them. This amazing bird plays like it is hurt and struggles in front of you with this "broken wing display" to lead you away when you get too close to its nest. It runs out about ten yards and flops around on the ground with one or both wings dragging, and when you start towards it, it moves out a ways and goes through the injury routine all over again. One of the pleasures of summer is seeing the killdeer chicks so far away from water and not on the ocean shore. Baby killdeers are born ready to run, and just as soon as the egg breaks they are searching for something to eat. They look like a "pair of legs only" when born, and I always wanted to add one to my pet list, but I never could catch one because I was always led away with the "broken wing show."

"I AM AN OLD MAN AND HAVE KNOWN A GREAT MANY TROUBLES, BUT MOST OF THEM NEVER HAPPENED."
—Mark Twain

 A LITTLE LAUGHTER: A piece of chewing gum with soap in it was a practical joke that I liked to play on family and friends. I would hollow out a piece of Dentine gum, because it was thicker, fill it with dish soap, and then wrap it back up and offer it to someone. It was the expression on their faces when they bit into the soap that made it worth the time. Dad's expression was always the best and he would always laugh, but I never would give it to Mother because I didn't think she could handle it. Both brothers were good sports and got the privilege of chewing the gum.

"IF YOU GO TO HEAVEN WITHOUT BEING NATURALLY QUALIFIED FOR IT, YOU WILL NOT ENJOY IT THERE."
—George Bernard Shaw

FIRE: "Will it fire?" Will the old Civil War cannon at the local cemetery fire or not? The old cannon had stood guard with old glory on top of the hill since the early 1900s, and we wanted to see it live again. A friend and I filled a can with cement that was the bullet, and the power was made from shotgun shells. A piece of dynamite fuse from the local hardware store was going to ignite it. "Light it and run," my buddy said. I lit the fuse and ran to a nearby tree to watch the fuse burn and disappear into the rusty old cannon. All was quiet and we were not so sure it was going to work. Then all of a sudden: "KA BOOM!" The cement can came out of the cannon so fast we could see nothing but smoke. CRASH, the tree growing about 20 feet in front of the cannon exploded in all directions. The sound was dreadful and we thought someone would come investigate, but they never did, and we were proud of ourselves for accomplishing our mission. The old cannon lived again!

"THE REASON WHY WORRY KILLS MORE PEOPLE THAN WORK IS THAT MORE PEOPLE WORRY THAN WORK."
—Robert Frost.

 TORNADO: It was May 25, 1955, when Mother woke me to a room full of people because of a tornado that had wiped out a small town south of us, called Udall. Dad was a ham operator, and he would spend hours talking to people worldwide. On this night it was the only communication there was into this city with no electricity, and the people were waiting for word from their loved ones. All had concerned looks on their faces while Mother served coffee and tried her best to make them feel as comfortable as she could. A few days after the tornado hit, I visited this small town and my last impression of the town was a car frame hanging in the only tree standing and the National Guard trucks with their red crosses. This picture was sent around the world by the Associated Press and became known as the famous "Tornado Alley."

"I THINK AND THINK FOR MONTHS, FOR YEARS. NINETY-NINE TIMES THE CONCLUSION IS FALSE. THE HUNDREDTH TIME I AM RIGHT."
—Albert Einstein

DEEP SEA FISHING: The waves were churning and higher than normal when the boat headed out to sea. This was the deep sea fishing trip I was on in Florida that traveled nine miles beyond the sight of land. The waves were tossing the small boat from side to side when we came to a stop, and the captain said, "Just bait the hook and let it drop to around 75 feet." So I baited the hook and "WOW," I caught a fish. We caught red snapper, sheep's head, sea bass, sting rays, an eel, and even a seagull that picked up the bait before it sank and was reeled around in the air before the line was cut. We all were concerned about the seagull, but it was OK and returned back to land with us. Seeing a shark's fin made me feel very vulnerable in such a small boat.

"USE YOUR HEALTH, EVEN TO THE POINT OF WEARING IT OUT. THAT IS WHAT IT IS FOR. SPEND ALL YOU HAVE BEFORE YOU DIE; DO NOT OUTLIVE YOURSELF."
—George Bernard Shaw

 IT DIDN'T COME EASY: My two brothers were exceptional and eventually became successful doctors within their own fields. Unfortunately, I wasn't gifted as my brothers, and Mother was constantly pushing me with homework with her encouraging words, "Do it again, it will come." Finally I realized that Mother's gift to me were those three little words, "Do it again," that have followed me throughout my life to be successful. Thanks, Mother, for your belief in your son and for your constant support.

"TO HAVE COURAGE FOR WHATEVER COMES IN LIFE –
EVERYTHING LIES IN THAT."
—Saint Teresa of Avila

ALL DRESSED IN WHITE: A state mental hospital, a children's ward, and a white uniform were the furthest from my dreams as means of working my way through college. But here I was in the midst of it all with physically handicapped, mentally challenged, and hopelessly ill children. These were the beautiful children of all ages that we hear stories about but never see. This work gave me strength and understanding that I needed to continue with life's work. God gave me this experience to carry me through the rest of my life. It was short-lived, but the memories are alive and live on inside of me.

"EVERYONE HAS HIS SUPERSTITIONS. ONE OF MINE HAS ALWAYS BEEN WHEN I STARTED TO GO ANYWHERE, OR TO DO ANYTHING, NEVER TO TURN BACK OR TO STOP UNTIL THE THING INTENDED WAS ACCOMPLISHED."
—Ulysses S. Grant

A MOMENT IN TIME: My college days were filled with enthusiasm and excitement in meeting new people. The memories of my hometown kept returning, and I thought, "I want to be back at the ol' swimming hole and the life that was so free from care on the farm." "I need to get with this game of learning," I kept telling myself. It was all part of growing up and I was homesick for my youth. Walking the railroad tracks as I did back on the farm gave me the same thoughts that I'd had as a boy – that the tracks would lead me out of the present into the future. A railroad track always seemed to follow me wherever I went, and I went back to walk the railroad track many years after graduation to see if I could remember the memories that I had of that time. The memories were quietly there and are now a gift of the future.

"DON'T BOTHER JUST TO BE BETTER THAN YOUR CONTEMPORARIES OR PREDECESSORS. TRY TO BE BETTER THAN YOURSELF."
—William Faulkner

 DEAL THE CARDS: "HAZING" was popular and traditional when I was attending college. This was during the good old days of staying out late, drinking beer, and above all playing jokes on the faculty. This was the time to be reminiscent of the movie *Animal House* and why my grades at the beginning of school suffered. My worst offense was to get called up to the "HILL," or to the administration building, to see the Academic Committee about my low grades. How embarrassing this was, and I still shudder thinking about it. Playing poker was more fun than studying, so up to the hill I was called to see why I was not making passing grades. All alone I sat outside these large tall double doors, waiting to be called inside to explain my grades. "I'm not going to make it," I said to myself. "I'm going to die before going in." The door finally swung open and in I went like a "lamb to slaughter." In front of me was a large horseshoe table with 12 professors, and I sat in the only chair before them – like a committee meeting in Washington, DC, when they want blood. The questioning began, and I soaked my shirt and my voice sounded like a soprano. The last question I was asked was "What reason do you think your grades are so low?" And I said, "Because I was playing poker." And the professor said, "I think they should have a poker championship and the winner gets kicked out of school!" After this embarrassing incident, I started studying and made the Dean's honor roll.

"COURAGE IS FEAR HOLDING ON A MINUTE LONGER."
—General George S. Patton

 FALL IN: The US Army was a different kind of schooling that I wasn't expecting in life. Vietnam was building up, and the training was in high gear to enlist as many men as possible. Unfortunately, I was one of the chosen to give some time and to come join them from the soft life of college. I found this way of life challenging to say the least. Three other college buddies and I enlisted to all be together, and we were sent to California for training. We signed up expecting to stay together, but only one of the four didn't stay with the others, and that was me. "Of all the luck," I thought. Well at least we all got sent together – that would soften the impact of going, so we boarded a train and headed for basic training in the Army. On the third day, we reached San Francisco and changed trains in the middle of the night to arrive at our destination at four a.m. in the morning. The drill instructor met us with this high-pitched voice and said, "I am your father now, and from now on your life belongs to the US Army." And it did!

"YOU GAIN STRENGTH, COURAGE AND CONFIDENCE BY EVERY EXPERIENCE IN WHICH YOU REALLY STOP TO LOOK FEAR IN THE FACE . . . YOU MUST DO THE THING YOU THINK YOU CANNOT DO."
—Eleanor Roosevelt

 WE ALL LOVED HER: After the Army, I met and married a wonderful woman and we had a beautiful daughter. We were all enjoying life when my wife passed unexpectedly at an early age. Forever with a smile on her face, she was the most positive individual that I have ever met. She was exceptional, she was special, she was beautiful, and she lived her life to the fullest. To accomplish both the father and mother roles is often difficult, but my daughter and I moved on with life where she'd left off. We all loved her and she will live in our hearts forever!

"THERE AIN'T NOTHING BUT ONE THING WRONG WITH EVERY ONE OF US, AND THAT'S SELFISHNESS."
—Will Rogers

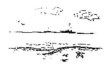 PRACTICE MAKES PERFECT: As a boy I was terrified of receiving shots or inoculations, and later in life became diabetic. The doctor said, "Son, you will have to take your daily shots for the rest of your life." Could I give myself shots every day? I would say to myself, "Yes, I can do it. It has to be done." It has been over thirty years and I have found the saying, "I can do it," words from my mother's insistence in school. We "all can do it" if we "all need to do it."

"INCHES MAKE A CHAMPION."
—Vince Lombardi

The most beautiful blue eyes I have ever seen, and she was our gift from heaven. She showed us strength and she demonstrated self-control after her mother's passing, and the pleasure she gave to us was overwhelming. Determination was her goal, to move forward with her life in the business world to become the best that she possibly could be in her profession. THE DIAMOND OF MY EYE ~ MY DAUGHTER!

"FROM THE MOMENT I PICKED UP YOUR BOOK UNTIL I LAID IT DOWN, I WAS CONVULSED WITH LAUGHTER. SOME DAY I INTEND TO READ IT."
—Groucho Marx

 KANSAS

THE OLD PLACE LOOKS THE SAME: Here I am at a class reunion and I see my old school has been replaced with a new one. This is where I saw my first aircraft fly over with the white jet contrails. The books had big pictures and the words were large and easy to read. I played my first sporting event here, and I saw my girlfriends with their long dresses and white stockings. The marble king "ruled the roost" and strutted his stuff while the loser went home with an empty marble sack. "I wasn't the king today, it wasn't me yesterday or all last week," I kept telling Mother, who was supplying my marbles. The ground was full of sandburs, and this was where I received my first nosebleed in a scuffle with the bully of the playground. "I think your boyfriend is a shrimp," I said to this girl and got slapped. I wanted her for myself but she was from the high-class part of town. This was the ground where I yelled at the top of my lungs at the enemy, "Com' on and get me if you think you're big enough." And he did!

"THE BEST AND MOST WONDERFUL THINGS IN THE WORLD CANNOT BE SEEN OR TOUCHED . . . THEY MUST BE FELT WITH THE HEART."
—Helen Keller

REMINISCING: The mascot eagle for my high school was three feet high and made out of concrete. It stood fearlessly guarding the front door of the high school rain or shine through all seasons. Every school had its opposition, and the rivalry between our school and other schools was lively. Many at our school wanted to punish other schools for coming to town and painting "our beloved bird." The mascot was constantly painted with different colors from other schools, and years later when the eagle was moved to the new high school, it was sanded down and the number of different colors of paint was sixteen. We knew which school color had the most layers because many of us carried scars from that school encounter.

"NEVER TO SUFFER WOULD HAVE BEEN NEVER TO HAVE
BEEN BLESSED."
—Edgar Allan Poe

 RECALLING OLD MEMORIES: Some of the rival schools were our adversaries. The other schools would beat us in sports or come to town and date our girls, so our high school boys would go paint their mascots and return with bruises, cuts, and broken fingers due to disagreements. Not once did I go with them, but I always encouraged them to go. "Let's go get them," I'd say. And then I would fade away and go home and get up the next morning to all kinds of abuse. They would all want to know what happened to me and why I didn't go with them, and I always had the "headache or cold" excuse.

AN ANGEL'S VISIT

"LOVE AND FAITH SEES THE INVISIBLE, FEELS THE INTANGIBLE AND ACHIEVES THE IMPOSSIBLE."
—Anonymous

AND THIS WAS MY HAPPENING.

A moonlit evening, and I had just gone to bed and was wide awake and listening to the freight train that was working its way up the track in the distance. While saying my prayers, I was suddenly aware of a presence in my room and rolled over to see what it was. The room was quiet with only the sound of breathing when something lit up the room with an intense white light. "OH MY GOD, whatever it is, it's COMING THRU THE WALL," and the room was illuminated with a visible reality. "What in the world is this? Whatever it is, it's coming thru the wall! Is this a dream?" This being had brought a feeling that I had never felt before. A feeling of INTENSE PURE LOVE! LOVE beyond physical words! My life was in the physical world, and what I was feeling gave me unbelievable LOVE beyond the imagination – LOVE that I could not describe. There was absolutely no fear in me of what I was seeing, and I welcomed it with all of my heart. This was done without speaking because its response to me was in PURE LOVE.

"DO THE THING YOU FEAR, AND THE DEATH OF FEAR IS CERTAIN."
—Ralph Waldo Emerson

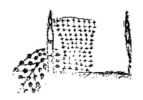

"IT'S MOVING, MY GOD IT'S MOVING" along the side of the bed, and I could see glowing balls of white light that were three rows deep and three rows wide, all moving in unison with a connection between each ball. They were energetic and intellectual and I wasn't frightened. I said out loud, "There is a swarm of bugs in here." What else was I to say seeing something like this? I didn't cover up my head or scream but stuck my hand out to catch one of the marching diamond-like objects, only to see them dart around my hand like fireflies with an intelligent manner. When I looked up to the front of the movement, it looked to be an incredible shining gown with the glowing balls moving in the trail of the gown.

"THE UNIVERSE IS FULL OF MAGICAL THINGS, PATIENTLY
WAITING FOR OUR WITS TO GROW SHARPER."
—Eden Phillpotts

Its goddess-like appearance was being revealed from another
dimension, and it was breathtakingly beautiful in its DIVINE way
with radiant gold and white blinding light. With a mystical air of
authority and astounding brilliance, it was proudly showing me all of
its incredible grandeur and heavenly splendor that it had brought
from the other side. Then I could feel that it was a female, and she
was wearing one of the most magnificent gowns that I had ever seen.
Why did I say "feel" that she was a female? Because of her elegant
gown and the way she moved, I could feel her presence as being
female. She didn't show her face, and she made me feel serene and
peaceful with nothing but LOVE from her. Her face was not visible,
and she seemed not to be showing it to me. She was hiding it from
me, and there was a reason for this that I will tell you later. Why was
she here, and was she showing me the life hereafter?

"WHATEVER COURSE YOU DECIDE UPON, THERE IS ALWAYS SOMEONE TO TELL YOU THAT YOU ARE WRONG. THERE ARE ALWAYS DIFFICULTIES ARISING WHICH TEMPT YOU TO BELIEVE THAT YOUR CRITICS ARE RIGHT. TO MAP OUT A COURSE OF ACTION AND FOLLOW IT TO AN END REQUIRES . . . COURAGE."
—Ralph Waldo Emerson

There was absolutely no fear in me from this breathtaking being. Existing in the physical world and then seeing something materialize in front of me was unthinkable. Was this really happening to me? I was sitting on the edge of the bed watching her go around my hands and arms. My eyes were wide open and my heart was pounding against my chest with LOVE FROM THE SPIRIT WORLD. I was on my feet, moving on the bedroom floor trying to catch these lighted balls of gold. She was unbelievable! Is this what some people have called "having an experience?" "Why me at this time of life? Com'on, this is going too far!" If this was a dream it was! A dream so real and vivid that my eyes were wide open in disbelief, seeing this incredible form in my home doing a pomp-and-circumstance march along my bed. Was this a miracle that we have all read so much about in the biblical days?

"GOD WILL NOT LOOK YOU OVER FOR MEDALS, DEGREES OR DIPLOMA, BUT FOR SCARS."
—Anonymous

My heart was beating so fast I thought it was going to burst. "What are these magnificent balls of light darting around, over and under my hands compared to something 'trying to catch your shadow'?" They moved around both sides of my body with quick movements. "Where did they come from?" I thought. To see inside of them reminded me of being back on the farm, holding up a newly born tadpole to the light and seeing its insides moving. This was a living intelligent life-form from another dimension.

"DON'T LEAVE BEFORE THE MIRACLE HAPPENS!"
Anonymous

THUD ~ ~ ~ SOMETHING HIT ME ON THE HEAD! She hit me on the head as I reached for one of those balls of light. It felt like a tingling softness, like electricity surrounding my head and body and rapidly running towards my heart. "What is this?" I thought. "What is going on here tonight?" My head went down to my chest in total pleasure! UNCONDITIONAL LOVE from the SPIRIT WORLD was running over my head and chest and moving quickly to emphasize my heart that had become overwhelmed with LOVE! This electrical energy stopped at my heart and felt like an anesthetic before an operation, but many times greater! This was SPIRIT LOVE like I'd never felt before. SPIRIT LOVE where I loved everything. No human words can explain this sensation that I had and the LOVE that was given to me from the SPIRIT world.

"THERE IS NOTHING THE BODY SUFFERS WHICH THE SOUL MAY NOT PROFIT BY."
—George Meredith

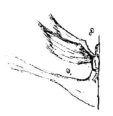

VANISHING: It was incredible seeing her movement towards the wall, and not stopping at the wall, but "STEPPING THRU THE WALL!" Yes, she stepped thru the wall. And I could see her complete body disappear to the other side with her long flowing gown still moving on this side. When she stepped thru to the other side, I could see an "opening in the wall" that closed up immediately after her like an invisible mirage. Droplets of gold that looked like teardrops were falling from the opening in the wall. She vanished as fast as she'd appeared; she had made her appearance known and then she was gone.

"ENDURANCE IS ONE OF THE MOST DIFFICULT DISCIPLINES, BUT IS TO THE ONE WHO ENDURES THAT THE FINAL VICTORY COMES."
—Buddha

Over and over again, I have relived this experience and visualized what I might have missed that night. When the trail of golden balls moved down to the end of the bed and turned the corner, I saw golden designs across her back. They looked to be crosses.

"OUR LIFE IS LIKE SOME VAST LAKE THAT IS SLOWLY FILLING WITH THE STREAM OF OUR YEARS. AS THE WATERS CREEP SURELY UPWARD, THE LANDMARKS OF THE PAST ARE ONE BY ONE SUBMERGED. BUT THERE SHALL ALWAYS BE MEMORY TO LIFT ITS HEAD ABOVE THE TIDE UNTIL THE LAKE IS OVERFLOWING."
—Alexandre Charles Auguste Bisson

Not in my wildest dreams would I have imagined writing this book, and it was written because I have been encouraged to do so. "Do it, the story needs to be written," I was told. "You need to let everyone know and be proud of this mystical happening." It may be difficult for you to believe in another life from another dimension and that we are the only ones living in the physical. For those of you who can comprehend another life, you may know what will be waiting for you as you grow older. Talking about my incident is emotional for me, and this book will authenticate my life to show you how normal I was growing up. When saying the Lord's Prayer the sentence, "On Earth as it is in Heaven," relates the two worlds, "Earth and Heaven." "Where is this heaven?" The other side is so close to us and she showed me how simple it was for her to step into our world. Only a veil separated us. Yes, this event happened, so be ready because one day it may happen to you!

"I'M A LITTLE WOUNDED, BUT I AM NOT SLAIN; I WILL LAY ME DOWN TO BLEED A WHILE. THEN I'LL RISE AND FIGHT AGAIN."
—John Dryden

My life has changed dramatically, both visibly and spiritually, from the very moment of this incredible encounter. Sometimes we may be blessed by experiences that seem to defy logic. My only wish now is to care for nature and to help serve mankind for the remainder of my life. This was a breathtaking vision that was given to me as an indication of what may be waiting for us. My eyes have seen the materialization of a SPIRIT from another dimension. If this love solution could be passed worldwide, there would be no wars. I wish for all mankind to feel this LOVE that is not a physical LOVE, but a "LOVE FROM THE SPIRIT WORLD."

"THE CREDIT BELONGS TO THE MAN WHO IS ACTUALLY IN THE ARENA; WHOSE FACE IS MARRED BY DUST AND SWEAT AND BLOOD; WHO STRIVES VALIANTLY; WHO ERRS AND COMES SHORT AGAIN AND AGAIN; WHO KNOWS THE GREAT ENTHUSIASMS, THE GREAT EMOTIONS, AND SPENDS HIMSELF IN A WORTHY CAUSE; WHO, AT THE BEST, KNOWS IN THE END THE TRIUMPH OF HIGH ACHIEVEMENT; AND WHO, AT THE WORST, IF HE FAILS, AT LEAST FAILS WHILE DARING GREATLY, SO THAT HIS PLACE SHALL NEVER BE WITH THOSE COLD AND TIMID SOULS WHO KNOW NEITHER VICTORY NOR DEFEAT."
—Theodore Roosevelt

NOT A DREAM: HER name is now known and why SHE appeared to me. My life is now fulfilled, knowing the answers that SHE gave me. GOD was to be awakened and strengthened in me, and I was to be receptive to it, seeing the life hereafter.

KNOWING GOD HAS BEEN A JOURNEY OF SPIRITUAL LOVE FOR ME.

"WHEN YOU GET TO THE END OF YOUR ROPE, TIE A KNOT AND HANG ON."
—Franklin Delano Roosevelt.

LEANING INTO THE WIND: What would you do if you had an experience like this happen to you? Who would you tell, or would you tell anyone? Would you share it with your closest friend, or would you keep it to yourself? I shared this experience with both of my brothers, who are doctors, and who gave me their undivided support.

"OUR MIND CANNOT POSSIBLY UNDERSTAND GOD. YOUR HEART ALREADY KNOWS. MINDS WERE DESIGNED FOR CARRYING OUT THE ORDERS OF THE HEART."
—Emmanuel

SEARCHING: Because of my strong belief in GOD, I turned to my faith for answers. Satisfying answers would be rewarding, but they continued to be unanswered. "Where do I turn from here?" I asked myself. Then I realized that I would have to continue the search until answers were found.

"THE BEST AND MOST BEAUTIFUL THINGS IN THE WORLD CANNOT BE SEEN OR TOUCHED . . . THEY MUST BE FELT WITH THE HEART."
—Helen Keller

THE JOURNEY: What an exhilarating journey this life has been for me. As I descend towards the final days I've had this incredible need to obtain answers concerning the other side. Yes, I must have the satisfaction of communicating with a medium.

"WHAT THE CATERPILLAR CALLS A TRAGEDY, THE MASTER CALLS A BUTTERFLY."
—Richard Bach

MY GUARDIAN ANGEL

GRACE: Immediately, the medium knew my visitor and that it wasn't a dream and actually happened as I have described it. HER NAME IS "GRACE," AND SHE IS A BEAUTIFUL DIVINE SPIRIT FROM THE SPIRIT WORLD. SHE IS MY GUARDIAN ANGEL.

"TRY NOT TO BECOME A MAN OF SUCCESS BUT RATHER TRY TO BECOME A MAN OF VALUE."
—Albert Einstein

CROSSING THE VEIL: Before I crossed the veil from the Spiritual to the Physical life to begin my life on earth, one of my themes that I was to experience on earth was that I was to write a book. GRACE stepped into my physical world from the Spirit World to jolt me into telling this story on how beautiful her world actually is on the other side with GOD, as well as to show me the LOVE that is waiting for us with welcoming arms and that the Spirit always lives. It's not fictional but true! She didn't show me her face because I was not to be connected to a certain Spirit, but to remember the meaning of her visit. Her purpose in showing me her magnificence was that I was at a level of spiritual vibration in life to accept her visit and could be encouraged to write about this event. Her name is popular in my world, and she made herself "visible" for me to remember that she will once again "step into" the physical world. Look for her and be ready to see her, and you may get to meet her because the veil between us is lifting. Trust me, when it happens, it will be the most stimulating event of your lifetime.

"TO FINISH THE MOMENT, TO FIND THE JOURNEY'S END IN EVERY STEP OF THE ROAD, TO LIVE THE GREATEST NUMBER OF GOOD HOURS, IS WISDOM."
—Ralph Waldo Emerson

See the SPIRIT! Know the SPIRIT! Feel the LOVE from the SPIRIT! Live your life to the fullest. We are but a whisper from the other world, and it is waiting for us with UNCONDITIONAL LOVE. My SPIRIT met and communicated with a heavenly SPIRIT, and it was exhilarating. The journey has been exciting, and this incredible vision has changed my life forever! AND I HAVE THE SENSE THAT MY SPIRITUAL ADVENTURE IS JUST BEGINNING!

Printed in the United States
127644LV00001B/62/P

9 781432 729233